essential
vegan
COOKBOOK

Banana Cake (see page 75)

essential vegan

COOKBOOK

Vanessa Almeida

This paperback edition was published in 2013 by Neni Design.

www.nenialmeida.com

Text copyright © 2013 by Vanessa Almeida
Photography copyright © 2013 by Neni Almeida

Design by Neni Almeida
Sub editing by Milo Steelefox
Ceramics by Luciene Calabria – see pages 16 and 21 and visit www.42pots.co.uk

A catalogue record for this book is available from the British Library.

ISBN 978-0-9926653-0-2

Printed in Great Britain by Butler Tanner & Dennis, UK

www.essentialvegan.co.uk

PREFACE

These delicious and compassionate recipes, gathered here in this book by Vanessa like precious gifts, fill our every day meals with beauty and harmony.

Her delicate blending of ingredients, combining the perfect aesthetic with wonderful and aromatic results, represents new chapters for the table of life.

Ahead of her time in her challenging of taboos, she brings together flavours and the appetite of the eye with the act of feeding oneself (and others) with consideration.

Vanessa herself, sensitive and "well seasoned", beautiful and nourishing, embellishes the chequered tablecloth of our days with unparalleled smells and flavours, and not a bland bite in sight in *Essential Vegan*, leaving us light of heart and with mouths watering. Bon appetite!

Regina Maria Amorim Vieira

CONTENTS

Breads 6
Salads 16
Starters 24
Side Dishes 32
Main Courses 40
Desserts 64
Snacks 88
Index by Health Tips 96

Basic Bread Loaf

- 500g strong white flour,
  plus extra for kneading
- 10g salt
- 14g dried active yeast
- 320ml cold water
- 40ml olive oil,
  plus extra for kneading

Nothing beats homemade bread. The bread machine in my home is my husband, Neni, who is also my photographer and designer – I know, multitasking husband. The smell and softness of this bread will blow your socks off. Try it – it's totally worth it.

Place the dry ingredients in a bowl, taking care not to have the salt and yeast touching.

Add the oil and 240ml of water.

Using your hands, mix the ingredients together. Gradually add the remaining water until all the flour leaves the side of the bowl and you have soft, rough dough.

Pour a little oil onto a clean work surface, then place the dough on the oil and begin to knead. Do this for 10 minutes.

Place the dough into a clean, oiled bowl. Cover with a damp cloth and leave it to rise in a warm place for 1 hour.

Once risen, place the dough onto a floured surface. Then proceed to knock the dough back by folding it in on itself repeatedly. Do this until all the air is coaxed out and the dough is smooth.

To shape into a bloomer, flatten the dough into a rectangle, and with the long side facing you, fold each end into the middle then roll it like a Swiss roll so that you have a smooth top with the seam along the base. Very gently roll with the heel of your hands.

Place the dough in a greased bread tin, cover and leave to prove for 1 hour at room temperature.

Lightly spray with water and dust with a little flour. Make four diagonal slashes using a sharp knife across the top.

Preheat the oven to 220°C and put a baking tray filled with water on the bottom shelf of the oven.

Place the loaf on the middle shelf and bake for 25 minutes.

After this time lower the heat to 200°C and bake for a further 10 minutes.

Remove from the oven and leave to cool on a wire rack.

Lavash Bread

- 75g flour
- 1/2 tsp sugar
- 1/2 tsp salt
- 1 tbsp vegan margarine melted
- 90ml lukewarm water
- 1 tbsp sesame seeds
- 1 tbsp lime seasoning
- 1 tbsp olive oil
- sea salt

SESAME SEEDS

Sesame seeds are a source of manganese, copper, calcium, magnesium, iron, phosphorus, vitamin B1, zinc and dietary fibre. They have been shown to have a cholesterol-lowering effect and have also been found to protect the liver from oxidative damage.

This is the most common bread in Armenia, Azerbaijan and Iran. It's so light and tasty, you won't quite believe it. This recipe gives you four lavash breads, but if you want more then just double the quantities. They're best when fresh and warm so make them on the day you intend to eat them. You can pretty much use any kind of seasoning you want - the sky's the limit.

In a large bowl mix together the flour, sugar, salt, sesame seeds and lime seasoning.

Pour in the melted margarine and warm water.

Using your hand, mix to a soft ball consistency.

Turn out onto a floured surface and knead for 5 minutes, and the dough should become smooth and elastic.

Divide the dough into 4 pieces and roll them into smooth balls.

Using a rolling pin open the dough out into circles about 2mm thick.

Bake them at 250°C for about 15 minutes or until golden brown.

Mix the olive oil with the sea salt and brush over the baked bread.

Homemade Focaccia

- 1 package dry yeast (7g)
- 1/3 cup warm water
- 2 ¼ cups cold water
- 5 tbsp olive oil
- 3 cups strong white bread flour
- 4 ½ cups all-purpose flour
- 1 tbsp salt
- sea salt
- 2 sticks of rosemary

ROSEMARY

Rosemary leaves contain certain phytochemical compounds that are known to have disease preventing and health promoting properties. The herb is exceptionally rich in many B-complex groups of vitamin, such as folic acid, pantothenic acid, pyridoxine and riboflavin.

This one might seem tricky but it just takes time - for most of it you're not actually doing anything, just waiting for the dough to prove. But it's all so worth the wait - this bread is simply divine!

Put the yeast in the warm water, stir and let it rest for 10 minutes.

Pour the 2 tablespoons of olive oil and cold water into a big bowl.

When the yeast has activated pour it into the water/oil mixture.

Whisk in 2 cups of flour and the salt and mix thoroughly.

Then, cup by cup, whisk in all the rest of the flour.

By the time you get to the last cup of flour, you will be able to work the dough with your hands.

On a floured surface, knead the dough for 8 minutes.

Transfer to a large clean bowl and spread 1 tablespoon of olive oil over the dough. Cover with cling film and leave it to prove (rise) for 1 ½ hours.

Divide the dough into two greased baking trays, cover it with cling film and leave to rest for another 30 minutes.

Dimple the bread with your thumbs and place the rosemary leaves in a few of the holes and set it to rest for another 2 hours.

When there's 30 minutes left to go, turn the oven on at 200°C.

Before placing the bread in the oven, drizzle a tablespoon of olive oil over each one and sprinkle on some sea salt.

Bake them both for 15 minutes or until golden brown.

Turn the loaves out onto a rack and leave them to cool.

If you're not going to eat it on the same day (though we advise you do!), best cover it with cling film.

Seeded Wholegrain Bread with Macadamia "Cheese"

- 500g strong wholegrain bread flour
- 1/4 cup sunflower seeds
- 1/4 cup sesame seeds
- 1/8 cup pistachio nuts
- 1 tsp fast action dried yeast
- 1 ½ tsp salt
- 25g vegan margarine
- 330ml lukewarm water
- 1 cup macadamia nuts
- 1/2 cup nutritional yeast
- 1 tsp salt
- 1 tsp garlic powder
- 1 tsp lemon and parsley seasoning
- 4 tbsp water
- 2 tbsp lemon juice

There's really nothing like the taste of homemade bread. This one smells heavenly and tastes ridiculously good. It's soft, rich, and can be a meal on its own quite frankly. The credit for this one has to go to my husband, Neni, as he was the one who did all the kneading and folding of the bread.

Two important tips to remember when baking a loaf of bread: 1) be sure to remove it from its tin and always place on a wire rack to cool down before cutting; 2) give the base of the loaf a firm *thump!* with your thumb, like striking a drum, and you'll find that the bread will sound hollow when it's done.

MACADAMIA NUTS

Macadamia nuts have a high level of monounsaturated fats and are a great source of protein. They contain all of the essential amino acids as well as some non-essential ones.

BREAD

Pulse the seeds in a food processor until ground well.

Mix the flour with the seeds.

In a big bowl mix together the seeded flour, yeast and salt. Add the margarine and rub in with your fingertips until the mixture resembles fine breadcrumbs.

Pour in the lukewarm water gradually so as to make a soft dough.

Transfer the dough to a lightly floured surface and knead for 12 minutes until the dough is smooth and elastic.

Put the dough in a big bowl, cover with cling film and leave it in a warm place for 1 hour to prove.

Tip the dough into a greased and floured 2lb loaf tin, cover and let it rest for another hour.

Bake it for 25 minutes in a preheated oven at 220°C.

MACADAMIA "CHEESE"

In a food processor blend the macadamia nuts, nutritional yeast, salt, garlic powder, water, seasoning and lemon juice for 3 minutes.

Albina's Calzone

- 1 cup almond milk
- 1 tbsp ground flaxseed
- 3 tbsp water
- 1 tbsp sugar
- 1 tbsp salt
- 30g biological yeast
- 2 tbsp vegan margarine
- 6 tbsp vegetable oil
- 3 cups flour
- 66g baby leaf spinach
- 110g green olives
- 10g pine nuts
- 10 cherry tomatoes halved
- 1 tbsp nutritional yeast
- salt
- black pepper

OLIVES

Olives are high in monounsaturated fat and vitamin E. They also contain polyphenols and flavonoids which have anti-inflammatory properties. The combination of these health-boosting elements allows olives to defend the heart against diseases and protect cells from free radicals.

Albina is my lovely grandmother, and an amazing cook. This family recipe was passed down from her to my mother, and now it's my turn, except that of course mine's a vegan version. You'll be glad to know that I've done it justice and kept the long-standing family tradition alive. Seriously though, this calzone *is* perfect: you can have it as a main dish, a starter, or slice it into a snack. Give it a shot, I guarantee you'll love it.

Mix the water and flaxseed and let it rest for 20 minutes.

Put the sugar and the biological yeast together and stir for a few minutes until it turns to liquid.

Combine the flour, margarine, milk and salt.

In a large bowl blend the flaxseed mixture and biological yeast liquid with the rest of the ingredients and make into a dough.

Cover the bowl and let it rest for 1 ½ hours.

In a small pan fry the onion until tender.

Add spinach, olives, pine nuts, tomatoes, nutritional yeast and seasoning, stir for 10 minutes.

On a floured surface open the dough to make one big calzone (or two medium-sized ones).

Spread the mixture in the middle of the dough and close it up.

Brush the calzone with olive oil and bake for 25 minutes at 200°C.

Brazilian "Cheese" Bread

- 455g potatoes, peeled and chopped
- 1/3 cup water plus water to boil the potatoes
- 2 cups tapioca flour
- 1/4 cup nutritional yeast
- 2 tsp salt
- 1/2 tsp baking powder
- 1/2 cup vegan cheese
- 1/3 cup vegetable oil

These Brazilian "cheese" breads are heavenly, and just like the real ones. Pão-de-queijo, as we called them in Brazil, are very popular, and are one thing I thought I was never going to eat again, but luckily for me and for you, we now have the perfect vegan recipe. You can keep the dough in the fridge for 2 days before baking, or freeze it as dough balls for up to 3 months.

In a small saucepan boil the water and cook the potatoes until tender, then drain and mash.

Preheat oven to 250°C, and line a baking tray with parchment paper.

In a small bowl mix the tapioca flour, nutritional yeast, salt and baking powder.

Then in a large bowl mix the cheese, 1/3 cup water and oil. Add the mashed potatoes and blend it all together.

Combine wet and dry ingredients to make a soft, smooth dough.

Mould small balls using your hands and transfer to the baking tray, then bake for 20 minutes or until puffed up and lightly golden.

TAPIOCA

Tapioca flour contains manganese, calcium, magnesium, phosphorus, zinc, copper and selenium. It's rich in carbohydrates and is considered a healthy starch as it's low in cholesterol and unhealthy fats, often used in dietary plans to promote weight gain. Given that it doesn't contain any gluten it's a healthier alternative to wheat flour, and both tapioca flour and tapioca starch can be used as a thickening agent in cream-based sauces and gravies.

Warm Conchigliette Salad with Garlic Bread

- *200g conchigliette pasta*
- *200g green beans*
- *2 courgettes*
- *2 carrots*
- *1/4 cup sunflower seeds*
- *4 tbsp teriyaki sauce*
- *4 tbsp olive oil*
- *2 tsp salt*
- *2 tsp paprika*
- *1 tsp mild chilli powder*
- *juice and zest of 1 lemon*
- *1 cup vegan cheese grated plus more to sprinkle*
- *2 small baguettes*
- *4 cloves of garlic smashed*
- *5g chives chopped*
- *4 tbsp vegan margarine*
- *smoked sea salt*

Serves 5

GREEN BEANS

Green beans contain healthy amounts of minerals like iron, calcium, magnesium, manganese, and potassium, which are most essential for body metabolism.

This recipe is Spring in a bowl. You can have it as a warm salad or a light meal. The vegetables are cooked yet crunchy, the pasta soft and the flavour of the sauce and lemon is just perfect. Garlic bread makes for the ideal accompaniment, adding to the array of flavours. I simply can't stress enough how good this is - you have to try it for yourself.

GARLIC BREAD

Crush together smashed garlic, chives, smoked sea salt, vegan margarine and vegan cheese, and mix it really well.

Place the baguettes on a chopping board and cut slits into them - not quite all the way through - enough to put in the filling but whilst keeping the bread intact.

Stuff the butter mixture into the gaps, then wrap the bread in tin foil and set aside.

Bake your garlic bread in the oven at 200°C for 25 minutes before serving - this is best done at the same time as you're cooking the pasta.

PASTA

Using a vegetable peeler slice the carrots and courgettes.

Mix the sliced vegetables with the fine beans, sunflower seeds, teriyaki sauce, olive oil, paprika and chilli powder and set to one side.

Cook the pasta in salted water as per the package instructions.

When done, add the vegetables, cover the pan and simmer over a low heat for 10 minutes. This will cook the vegetables a bit but not entirely, so that they retain their crunchiness.

Add the lemon juice and zest and serve.

Black Eyed Beans Salad

- *235g black eyed beans*
- *1/2 onion thinly chopped*
- *10g chives chopped*
- *10g parsley chopped*
- *12 cherry tomatoes quartered*
- *1/4 cup olive oil*
- *juice of 1 lime*
- *2 tbsp smoked sea salt flakes*

Serves 4

BLACK EYED BEANS

These are a good source of heart-supporting nutrients such as folate, magnesium, iron, and potassium, that help to lower cholesterol, triglycerides and blood pressure.

This is one of the easiest salads ever and is also super healthy. I use black eyed beans but it works well with most kinds.

If short on time, it's OK to use canned beans, just be sure to wash them first. Worth noting too that the dish tastes better if you leave it in the fridge for 30 minutes before serving.

Wash the beans in a colander and cook if necessary.

Add the onions, tomatoes and chives and mix well.

Add the olive oil, lime juice and salt.

Place in the fridge to chill.

Potato Salad

- 500g mini new potatoes halved
- 5 tbsp raisins
- 1/2 onion chopped
- 35g carrots sliced
- 2 tbsp olive oil
- 1 tbsp mustard
- 2 sticks of spring onion chopped
- 3/4 cup of vegan mayonnaise
- salt
- black pepper

Serves 4

RAISINS

The health benefits of raisins include relief from constipation, anemia and fever. Raisins also help with weight gain, eye care, dental care, and bone health. They are a good source of antioxidants, and the vitamins K, C, E and B.

This salad is ideal for a picnic on a warm Spring day. It goes wonderfully with leaves of any kind - I like to make it with rocket but you can go with whatever takes your fancy.

Boil the potatoes for 20 minutes.

Drain the water off and let them cool.

In a bowl mix the potatoes with the rest of the ingredients and place in the fridge for 25 minutes before serving.

Yogurt and Melon Salad

- 5 tbsp vegan plain yogurt
- 1 tbsp olive oil
- juice of 1/2 lemon
- zest of 1 lemon
- 1/2 tbsp smoked sea salt
- 10g chives chopped
- 200g lettuce
- 100g rocket
- 1 tsp paprika
- 100g sun blushed tomatoes
- 140g melon

Serves 3

This salad is so simple and quick to prepare, yet it still finds the time to be most delicious! Perfect as a starter, or better still as a light meal on a really hot day.

Mix the yogurt, lime juice and zest, olive oil, salt and chives and set aside.

Cut the melon into small squares or balls.

Mix the lettuce, rocket, sun blushed tomatoes, paprika and melon and drizzle with olive oil.

Pour on the yogurt dressing and serve.

MELON

Melons are, among other things, an important source of vitamin C, which is an antioxidant that plays an important role in the growth and maintenance of all tissues in your body, namely in the healing of wounds and the repair of cartilage, bones and teeth.

Quinoa Tabouli Salad

- 150g washed and cooked quinoa
- 2 cloves of garlic smashed
- juice and zest of 1 lemon
- 1 cucumber diced
- 10 cherry tomatoes quartered
- 10g parsley chopped
- 1 avocado cut into cubes
- 1 tbsp olive oil
- smoked sea salt

Serves 4

Tabouli (or Tabbouleh) is so revitalising and makes for a perfect summer salad. As you'll see below it's best to mix the vegetables first *then* add the quinoa - this is because if you *don't* the quinoa absorbs all the dressing and leaves the vegetables a bit tasteless.

Mix together the garlic, lemon juice and zest, cucumber, tomatoes, avocado, parsley and salt in a salad bowl.

Add the quinoa and mix well with the vegetables.

AVOCADO

Avocados are considered one of the healthiest foods on the planet because they contain in excess of 25 essential nutrients, including vitamins A, B, C, E, and K, copper, iron, phosphorus, magnesium, and potassium. They also contain fibre, protein, and several beneficial phytochemicals such as beta-sitosterol, glutathione and lutein, which may protect against various diseases and illnesses.

Quinoa Tofu Salad

- 1 cup of quinoa
- 2 cups of water
- 2 tbsp olive oil
- 2 cloves of garlic smashed
- 200g smoked tofu cut into small cubes
- juice and zest of 1 orange
- salt
- black pepper

Serves 4

QUINOA

Quinoa has become highly appreciated for its nutritional value as it's a source of complete protein. It is also a very good source of fibre, calcium and phosphorus, and if that's not good enough quinoa is also high in magnesium and iron. It's very useful for a vegan diet or just for people looking for a nutritional and healthy meal.

This salad is really refreshing and ultra healthy, naturally. It takes no time to prepare and is simply scrumptious.

Firstly, wash the quinoa thoroughly in running water, otherwise it can become a little bitter in taste.

Then cook the quinoa in a saucepan with the water for 15 minutes.

When ready transfer to a big bowl and pour on 1 tbsp of the olive oil and the orange zest and set aside.

Fry the garlic with the rest of the olive oil.

Add the tofu, salt, black pepper and the orange juice and stir for 2 minutes.

Pour the mixture over the quinoa and mix together.

Leave in the fridge for 30 minutes before serving.

Shimeji Gyoza

- 1 ½ cups flour
- 1/2 cup lukewarm water
- 150g shimeji mushrooms
- 1/2 onion chopped
- 3 sticks of spring onion chopped
- 1 tbsp sesame seeds
- 2 tbsp soya sauce
- 4 ½ tbsp sesame oil
- 1 tbsp parsley and lemon seasoning
- salt
- black pepper

Serves 3

SHIMEJI

Shimeji contains beta-glucans which are a successful remedy for retarding and destroying growing tumours. The mushrooms can also help diabetes, asthma and certain allergies by enhancing the immune system and boosting its healing capabilities.

OK, I know this recipe sounds a little complicated and fiddly but it's actually not. The dumplings are so tasty that it's totally worth the time you spend in the kitchen. The dough is light and easy to prepare and the sesame oil makes all the difference. So give it a go, you'll thank me later!

Mix the water and the flour into dough.

Put a wet cloth over the dough, and let it rest for 15 minutes.

Divide the dough into 18 pieces of around 1 x 1.5cm in size.

Fry the onions until tender, add the rest of the ingredients and only 1/2 a tbsp of sesame oil. Stir for about 10 minutes.

Using a rolling pin open the dough pieces out and make them as round as possible.

Divide the shimeji mixture into the pastry circles placing about 1 tbsp in the middle of each one.

Fold wrappers in half over filling and pinch it shut in the centre.

Hold the wrapper in the middle spot that you just pinched with one hand, and make a pleat in the top part of the wrapper, pinching it against the flat edge at the back.

Holding the filled half-circle in the one hand, pleat the top of the wrapper from the middle out, continuing to press it to the flat edge. Proceed to make two or three more pleats either side of the first one to seal it all up.

Then boil them, just as you would regular pasta, and the steam cooks the pillows until they all reach the surface.

Using the rest of the sesame oil fry the dumplings, 2 minutes each side or until golden brown, and serve them with soya sauce.

Marinated Aubergines

- 2 aubergines sliced
- 3 cloves of garlic
- 1 onion thinly chopped
- 1/2 cup pine nuts
- 1/2 cup raisins
- 1 vegetable stock cube
- 2 tbsp olive oil
- black pepper

Serves 4

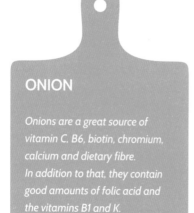

ONION

*Onions are a great source of vitamin C, B6, biotin, chromium, calcium and dietary fibre.
In addition to that, they contain good amounts of folic acid and the vitamins B1 and K.*

This is an old recipe that my mum's been making since, well, forever. It's perfect with crackers but you can also use it as a pastry filling or with salad. Always best from the second day onwards, if you leave it to marinate in the fridge the flavours blend together wonderfully and the end result is just delicious.

Boil the aubergine for 15 minutes to lose its water, then drain and set aside.

Fry the onions and garlic in some oil until tender.

Add the rest of the ingredients apart from the 2 tablespoons of olive oil and cook it all steadily for 20 minutes.

Turn off the heat and then add the olive oil, and let it cool completely before placing it in the fridge to marinate.

Sausage Rolls with no sausage

- 1 sheet puff pastry
- 500g closed cup chestnut mushrooms sliced
- 4 cloves of garlic smashed
- 1 onion chopped
- 3 sticks of spring onion chopped
- 15 cherry tomatoes halved
- 10g chives chopped
- 1 carrot diced
- 227g pineapple pieces in fruit juice
- 6 tbsp breadcrumbs
- 2 tbsp nutritional yeast
- salt
- black pepper
- 2 tbsp vegan margarine melted
- black sesame seeds

Serves 4

CARROT

Carrots are rich in beta-carotene, which is converted into vitamin A in the liver. Vitamin A is transformed in the retina to rhodopsin, a purple pigment necessary for night vision. Beta-carotene has also been shown to protect against macular degeneration and senile cataracts. The high level of beta-carotene acts as an antioxidant to cell damage done to the body through regular metabolism. It helps slow down the aging of cells and is a powerful antiseptic.

My version of the classic party food: vegan of course, and not a sausage in sight. What?? Nope, I didn't want to use the ready-made vegan sausages that you can buy in the supermarket, and went for a healthier, and in my opinion tastier version too! This is easy to prepare and you end up with around 20 rolls, ideal for when you have guests or want something different for dinner. We had it with salad and it went down a treat! Oh, and a tip for you: these are best served at room temperature.

Fry the garlic and onion until tender.

Add the mushrooms and cook for about 7 minutes stirring from time to time.

Add the carrots, chives, tomatoes, spring onions, salt and black pepper and cook for another 5 minutes.

Pour in the pineapple and keep stirring for another 5 minutes.

Remove from the heat and add the breadcrumbs and nutritional yeast.

On a floured surface cut the puff pastry into two long rectangles.

Place a layer of the mushroom mixture down the middle of each pastry rectangle, and then brush each side with melted vegan margarine.

Fold the other side of the pastry over, press down to seal and trim off any excess.

Brush the top with the rest of the melted margarine and sprinkle the sesame seeds on top.

Bake for 30 minutes in a preheated oven at 180°C.

Let them cool and cut each pastry roll into 8-10 small rolls.

Crispy Tofu Pillows

- 4 sheets filo pastry
- 400g tofu
- 2 tbsp teriyaki sauce
- 3 tbsp olive oil
- 15g chives chopped
- 2 cloves of garlic smashed
- 1/2 onion chopped
- 2 tsp paprika
- 1/2 tbsp liquid smoke
- 2 tsp chilli powder
- juice and zest of 1 lemon
- salt
- black pepper

Serves 4

PAPRIKA

Paprika's top benefit is that it is extremely high in vitamin C. A whole paprika pepper is known to have six to nine times the amount of vitamin C as a tomato. Because of this high content, paprika can also help you absorb iron-rich foods and may help your body fight common infections.

This is so easy and yet so delicious, you just have to try it. It goes really well with salad and couscous. The filo sheets are extremely delicate and dry up pretty quick so remove them from the package only when you are ready to start, otherwise place a wet kitchen towel on top of them. All of the preparation takes about 40 minutes, including marinating time, so this makes for a quick and yummy lunch or dinner. Give it a go, I guarantee you'll love it!

Freeze the tofu, first of all.

The day before, take the tofu out of the freezer and leave it in the fridge overnight to defrost, or simply place in hot water for 2 hours.

Squeeze the tofu until you drain all of the water out of it. You might be surprised how much water comes out, and it'll feel rather like a sponge.

Crumble the tofu with your fingers until it becomes granulated.

In a bowl mix the tofu with the rest of the ingredients and let it marinate for about 30 minutes.

Lay out a filo sheet, place a 1/4 of the tofu mixture in the middle, then roll it up tightly into a pillow shape, and tuck in the edge to seal. Repeat the process until you have four pillows.

Fry it, without oil, for about 2 minutes each side or until crispy and golden brown.

Tomato and Parsley Tartlets

- 85g vegan margarine
- 160g all-purpose flour
- 1/2 onion chopped
- 20g parsley chopped
- 12 plum tomatoes quartered
- 20g pine nuts
- 1 vegetable stock cube
- 200g vegan single cream

Serves 4

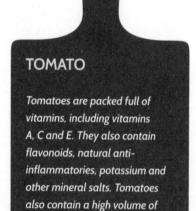

TOMATO

Tomatoes are packed full of vitamins, including vitamins A, C and E. They also contain flavonoids, natural anti-inflammatories, potassium and other mineral salts. Tomatoes also contain a high volume of water and are low in calories too.

These tartlets are simply delish, and you can serve them cold as canapés or hot as an accompaniment to your meal. Either way they're just lovely!

In a small bowl mix the margarine and the flour into a dough.

Divide the dough evenly and open it out across all the spaces of a greased muffin tin and bake at 180°C for 20 minutes or until they start to brown.

Remove the tartlet shells and set aside.

In a small pan fry the onions until tender.

Add the tomatoes, parsley, vegetable stock and pine nuts and stir for about 10 minutes.

Pour in the single cream and mix well with the rest of the ingredients.

Place the mixture on the tartlet shells and serve.

Savoury Profiteroles

Profiteroles
- *3 tbsp ground flaxseed*
- *9 tbsp water*
- *60g vegan margarine*
- *3/4 cup water*
- *3/4 cup plain flour*

Aubergine filling - see page 26

Sauce
- *150ml vegan single cream*
- *juice of 1 lemon*
- *5g chives chopped*
- *1/2 tsp paprika*
- *1/2 tbsp smoked sea salt*

Serves 4

Sophisticated yet simple, this dish is light but full of flavour and different textures. Serve them as a starter at a dinner party and I bet your friends will be impressed.

PROFITEROLES

Mix the flaxseed with the 9 tablespoons of water and let it set for 15 minutes.

In the meantime bring the water and margarine to the boil in a small saucepan.

Add flour and mix vigorously with a wooden spoon until the mixture comes away from the sides and forms a ball. This should only take a few seconds.

Transfer the dough to a mixing bowl, add the flaxseed mixture and beat with an electric mixer until glossy and smooth.

Pipe 12 little dollops of pastry out onto a parchment-lined cookie tray about 1 inch apart and bake for 15 minutes at 200°C.

FILLING

Marinated Aubergines, see page 26

SAUCE

Mix all the ingredients together.

PUTTING YOUR STARTER TOGETHER

Open the profiteroles with a knife.

Put one teaspoon of the marinated aubergines inside each one.

In a small bowl pour 2 tablespoons of the sauce and place three profiteroles on top of the sauce and serve.

CHIVES

Chives are very low in calories; they contain many noteworthy flavonoid anti-oxidants, plant fibre, minerals, and vitamins that have proven health benefits.

Courgette Balls

- *2 courgettes grated*
- *1/2 onion thinly chopped*
- *100g smoked tofu cut into tiny cubes*
- *1 handful baby leaf spinach chopped*
- *3 tbsp flour*
- *black pepper*
- *salt*

Serves 4

COURGETTE

A cup of cooked courgette contains only 16 calories and virtually no saturated fat. Of the fat that it does contain, most of it comes from omega-3 fatty acids, which are associated with stabilising "bad cholesterol." It is also a source of amino acids like phenylalanine and cystine, making it useful for vegans and vegetarians looking to build complete proteins by combining foods.

These balls have a great combination of textures: smooth on the inside and crispy on the outside. When making them it might seem as if they're not going to hold together, but fret not - they *will* stick, and go wonderfully with rice and salad.

Boil the courgette for about 15 minutes to lose its water.

Make sure you then drain most of the water out after doing so.

Mix the boiled courgettes with the rest of the ingredients and smash it all up with a fork.

Using your hands make small balls and place them on a baking tray covered with baking paper and put them in at 180°C for 30-35 minutes or until golden brown.

Red Lentil Mash

- 1 ½ cups of red lentils
- 60ml vegan single cream
- 1 tsp salt

Serves 4

RED LENTILS

Red lentils help to lower cholesterol, manage blood-sugar disorders and provide vitamins, minerals and protein with virtually no fat, and are very low in calories. They are also an important source of protein: a 1 cup serving of lentils provides nearly 40% of your daily recommended intake of protein.

This recipe is so easy and quick that there's really no excuse for not trying it out. It's lighter than regular mashed potato and healthier too - super simple yet so very tasty - you'll see...

Cook the lentils for a bit longer than you would normally do so, for about 15 minutes.

Mash them up until smooth.

Add the single cream and the salt and mix it all together well.

Rice Cakes

- 350g cooked brown rice
- 1 can of peas
- 1 onion chopped
- 100g sun-blushed tomatoes diced
- 5 tbsp olive oil
- 1 tbsp flour
- 3/4 cup of breadcrumbs
- 1/4 cup nutritional yeast
- 10g of parsley chopped
- salt
- black pepper

Serves 5

We all like a good rice cake, right? To make these I use peas and sun-blushed tomatoes and that makes all the difference. You can deep fry them if you want but there's no need to as they get nice and crispy in the oven anyway. They're super tasty and make for the perfect accompaniment to a salad.

In a big bowl combine all the ingredients together.

Make small balls with your hands and place them on a baking tray covered with a sheet of baking paper.

Bake for 25 minutes at 200°C.

BROWN RICE

A good source of selenium, fibre and manganese. It's rich in naturally-occurring oils, promotes weight loss, is proven to reduce the buildup of arterial plaque and also the risk of heart disease and high cholesterol. It helps stabilise blood sugar levels and is rich in anti-oxidants too.

Stuffed Portobello Mushrooms

- 400g mini Portobello mushrooms
- 1/2 onion chopped
- 4 cloves of garlic diced
- 5g chives chopped
- 1 tbsp nutritional yeast
- 2 tbsp breadcrumbs
- vegetable oil
- salt
- black pepper

Serves 3

PORTOBELLO MUSHROOMS

Besides being very tasty indeed, these are ultra nutritious. They're a good source of nutrients, such as copper, folate and niacin, and have as much potassium as a banana, which is essential for a healthy heart. On top of that they're also a source of calcium.

This recipe is delicious, and you can serve it as an appetiser or as a side dish - however you fancy, it's good, heavenly so.

Take 2/3 of the mushrooms, sprinkle on a little bit of salt and set them to one side, before slicing the rest of them.

Sauté the onions and garlic in a little vegetable oil until tender.

Add the sliced mushrooms, chives, salt and pepper and cook for 15 minutes over a low heat.

Turn off the heat and add the nutritional yeast and breadcrumbs.

In a non-stick frying pan fry the Portobello mushrooms you set aside at the beginning (no need for oil) for 2 minutes on each side.

When ready, stuff the fried mushrooms with the cooked mixture and serve straight away.

Potato Dauphinoise

- *700g potatoes sliced*
- *1 red onion chopped*
- *500ml vegan single cream*
- *1 tbsp nutritional yeast*
- *4 sticks of spring onion chopped*
- *1 vegetable stock cube*
- *20g vegan cheese grated (optional)*
- *salt*
- *black pepper*

Serves 6

POTATO

Potatoes are nutrient-dense, meaning you get a lot of nutrients for the amount of calories they have. The fibre is half soluble, half insoluble, so it helps to keep you regular and to lower cholesterol, and slowing down digestion helps to keep you full for longer. They also help lower blood pressure and are very high in potassium, iron and copper, too.

This dish is really rather lovely – surely the ultimate comfort food! The combination of potato and cream is perfect. Try it with rice and salad, it'll work a treat.

Cook the potatoes in salted water for 15 minutes.

Fry the onions in vegetable oil until tender.

Add the spring onions, vegetable stock, nutritional yeast, vegan cheese and black pepper and stir for 5 minutes.

Pour in the vegan single cream and stir for a further 2 minutes.

Transfer the potatoes to a baking tray and pour the cream on top of them.

Bake for 30 minutes in a preheated oven at 180°C.

Broccoli with Cashew

- 160g broccoli florets
- 4 cloves of garlic smashed
- 1/4 cup cashew nuts
- 1 tbsp olive oil
- sea salt

Serves 2

This recipe couldn't be easier, but it's full of nutrients and tastes really good. Give it a whirl, it'll be ready within 5 minutes and you'll love it not just for that!

In a frying pan fry the garlic in the oil until tender.

Toss the cashews in and cook them until they begin to brown.

Add the broccoli florets, stir for 4 minutes and serve while still hot.

BROCCOLI

Broccoli is a good source of vitamins C and A, folic acid and fibre. It regulates blood pressure, and this is made possible because of the presence of magnesium, calcium and potassium in it. The high content of potassium is also attributed to maintaining a healthy nervous system, and it also works in promoting the regular growth of muscles.

Vegetable Tart

- 200g plain flour
- 130g vegan margarine
- 150g butternut squash diced
- 150g sweet potato diced
- 1 red onion chopped
- 1 carrot diced
- 15 mini new potatoes halved
- 1 vegetable stock cube
- 2 sticks of spring onion chopped
- salt
- black pepper

Serves 6

RED ONION

Red onions are one of the best natural sources of quercetin, a bioflavonoid that is particularly well-suited for scavenging free radicals. Aside from its antioxidant properties, quercetin has been found to possess cancer fighting, anti-fungal, anti-bacterial, and anti-inflammatory properties.

This dish is an elegant one and it goes really well with rice, salad, or whatever you fancy. It's a regular at home and I can guarantee it'll start popping up a lot in your kitchen too.

In a bowl mix the vegan margarine and the flour. Use your hands to bring together into dough. Add a little more flour if the dough seems sticky, but be careful not to make the mixture too dry.

Open the dough out in a greased 24cm round springform baking pan (one with sides about 1cm high).

In a frying pan fry the onion until tender.

Add the rest of the ingredients and stir for 15 minutes or until the vegetables begin to get tender too.

Transfer and arrange the vegetables on the dough in the pan and bake for 25 minutes in a preheated oven at 180°C.

Mushroom Roast

- 250g closed cup chestnut mushrooms sliced
- 3 cloves of garlic smashed
- 1/2 onion chopped
- 3 sticks of spring onion chopped
- 10 cherry tomatoes halved
- a handful of chives chopped
- 1 carrot diced
- 227g pineapple pieces in fruit juice
- 113g breadcrumbs
- salt
- black pepper

Serves 6

PINEAPPLE

Pineapples are packed with vitamins and minerals, from vitamins A and C to calcium, phosphorus and potassium. On top of that they're also rich in fibre and calories, yet low in fat and cholesterol. All the nutrients it contains promote good health.

I've been doing this recipe for over 5 years and it's one of our favourites - I've added and removed ingredients along the way and it just gets ever better. Pineapple for example gives it a sweet taste that adds a different edge. Serve it with some salad and couscous and you have a perfectly-balanced meal.

Fry the garlic and onion until tender.

Add the mushrooms and cook for about 7 minutes stirring every now and again.

Pop the carrots, chives, tomatoes, spring onion, salt and black pepper in too and cook for 5 minutes.

Add the pineapple and keep stirring for a further 5 minutes.

Remove from the heat and add the breadcrumbs.

Pour the mixture out onto a greased baking tray and arrange it with your hands to get it nice and even.

Bake for 30 minutes in a preheated oven at 180°C.

Pine Nuts and Lemon Rice

- 300g brown rice
- 1/2 onion chopped
- 3 cloves of garlic smashed
- 3 tbsp pine nuts
- 10g chives chopped
- 10g parsley chopped
- 200g tofu
- 2 tbsp olive oil
- juice and zest of 2 lemons
- 200g vegan single cream
- 1/2 tsp paprika
- smoked sea salt

Serves 5

LEMON

Lemon is strong in the antiviral, antibacterial and immune-boosting departments, helping with weight loss, digestion and cleansing the liver, containing citric acid, magnesium, calcium, vitamin C, bioflavonoids, pectin, and limonene.

Light and refreshing, this recipe is a perfect meal for a warm day, and if you fancy turning it into a more substantial risotto just substitute the brown rice for Arborio rice, and voilà.

Fry the onion and garlic until tender.

Cook the rice as per the instructions on the packet.

When you add water to the rice for the last time put the pine nuts and parsley in too.

In a small bowl crumble the tofu and add the olive oil, salt, and juice and zest of one of the lemons.

When the rice is ready mix it in well with the tofu.

In a separate bowl blend the single cream with the chives, paprika, smoked sea salt, and the remaining lemon juice and zest.

Serve the sauce together with the rice.

Lentil Burgers

- 250g cooked brown lentils
- 2 carrots grated
- 1/2 onion chopped
- 1/2 cup flour
- 1 tbsp lemon and parsley seasoning
- sea salt
- black pepper
- 1 tbsp olive oil

Serves 5

LENTILS

Iron and folic acids are two important nutrients that help to build the red blood cells in your body. They are easily found in animal products so as vegans we need to look elsewhere to make sure we get enough and on a regular basis, and lentils are a very good source of both of them.

A handy tip for you for this dish: when cooking the lentils, which takes around 30 minutes, make sure you don't put any salt in as this will stop them from softening up properly.

Other than that, the ingredients in this burger recipe stick together a treat, and their flavour is rather amazing too.

Take a large mixing bowl and combine all the ingredients thoroughly, even mash it a bit so it all sticks together nicely.

Make each burger out of 2 tablespoons of the mixture and shape them with your hands.

Bake them for 45 minutes in a preheated oven at 180°C.

Be sure to turn the burgers over half way through so as to get an even brown colour on both sides.

Tofu Steak with Fried Onion

- 400g firm tofu cut into 1cm slices
- 1/2 cup light soy sauce or teriyaki sauce
- 2 cloves of garlic smashed
- 1 tbsp sea salt
- 5 tbsp olive oil
- 1 tsp paprika
- 1 tsp chilli powder
- a few sprays of liquid smoke
- 1 onion cut into chunky slices
- vegetable oil

Serves 3

TOFU

Tofu is a very good source of protein, soy protein specifically. Research on this in recent years has shown that regular intake of soy protein can help to lower total cholesterol levels by as much as 30%, to lower LDL (bad cholesterol) levels by as much as 35-40%, to lower triglyceride levels and reduce the tendency of platelets to form blood clots, and possibly even to raise levels of HDL (good cholesterol).

If you are not a number 1 fan of tofu, as I am, this recipe will do the trick. These fillets are heavenly: the saltiness of the sauce together with the sweetness of the fried onion is just great. Give it a go, you'll be amazed (and converted), I'm sure!

On a baking tray combine all the ingredients apart from the tofu and the onions, and mix it all thoroughly.

Then add the tofu and let it marinate in the fridge for anything from 2 to 24 hours. In this case, the longer you can leave it, the better.

Heat a frying pan with a little bit of vegetable oil and fry the tofu slices, three at a time, until golden brown. Repeat the process until all the tofu slices are nicely done.

Once you've fried the tofu, add a bit more vegetable oil to the frying pan, add the sauce of your choice too and fry the onions until soft.

Spread the onions on top of the tofu fillets and serve straight away.

"Cheesy" Quiche

- 200g flour
- 110g vegan margarine
- 215g tofu
- 1 tsp balsamic vinegar
- 1 onion chopped
- 250ml vegan single cream
- 50g vegan cheese grated
- 1 tbsp lemon parsley seasoning
- 1 vegetable stock cube
- 1 tbsp olive oil

Serves 6

BALSAMIC VINEGAR

Balsamic vinegar works to suppress the body's appetite and increase the amount of time it takes for the stomach to empty, which can contribute to weight loss by preventing overeating. According to Nutrition Data, balsamic vinegar is a source of calcium, iron, manganese and potassium, which all improve the body's functioning and weight loss capacity.

I absolutely love a challenge, and like to veganise every recipe I used to prepare before I became a vegan. It's good to know that if you want to, you can prepare your old recipes and they will taste *as good as*, if not *significantly better* than they did so before. This quiche is lovely and makes for a great evening meal. Take on the challenge, and enjoy the result!

Using your fingers bring the flour and margarine together into a dough.

Open the dough on an 8 inch round springform baking tray.

Fry the onion in the vegetable oil over a low heat for about 5 minutes, stirring from time to time.

Squeeze the block of tofu between your hands to get some of the liquid out (press it under a weighty object beforehand if you have time), and then crumble it into small pieces with your fingers.

Add the tofu, seasoning, balsamic vinegar and vegetable stock and stir for about 5 minutes.

Pour in the single cream and add the vegan cheese and stir for another 2 minutes.

Transfer the mixture to the baking tray and cook it for 30 minutes at 180°C.

Tofu Minced Meat

- 300g tofu
- 2 tbsp soya sauce
- 1 tbsp olive oil
- 15g parsley chopped
- 2 cloves of garlic smashed
- 1/2 onion chopped
- lemon juice
- 10 plum tomatoes halved
- 70g pineapple pieces
- salt
- black pepper
- 3 tbsp vegetable oil

Serves 4

PARSLEY

Parsley is rich in many vital vitamins, including vitamins A, B12, C and K. This means parsley helps keep your immune system strong, tone your bones and heal the nervous system too.

Tofu on its own can be a touch bland, but it has an enormous facility with absorbing the flavour of anything you mix it with. In this recipe we freeze the tofu so we can 1) change its texture, and 2) in defrosting it, enhance its capacity to absorb.

Freeze the tofu, first of all.

Remove the tofu from the freezer and leave it in the fridge overnight, or alternatively place in hot water for 2 hours.

Squeeze the tofu until you drain the water out of it - it should feel somewhat sponge-like.

Break the tofu up with your fingers until it becomes granulated.

In a bowl mix the tofu with the soya sauce, lemon juice, olive oil, black pepper and salt, and set aside.

Heat the vegetable oil and fry the garlic and the onion until tender.

Pour in the tofu mixture and stir for about 15 minutes or until it starts to brown a little.

Add the tomatoes, parsley and pineapple pieces, stir for another 5 minutes, and serve.

Tomato and Leek Quiche

Quiche base
- 110g vegan margarine
- 200g flour

Filling
- 1/2 onion chopped
- 4 cloves of garlic smashed
- 80g leek sliced
- 8 cherry tomatoes halved
- 1 handful of pine nuts
- 250ml vegan single cream
- 2 sticks of spring onion chopped
- 1 vegetable stock cube
- black pepper to taste

Serves 4

LEEK

Leeks are a great source of minerals and vitamins that are essential for optimum health. Their leafy stems contain several vital vitamins such as pyridoxine, folic acid, niacin, riboflavin and thiamin, all in very healthy proportions.

Quiche is something I always cook - it doesn't take at all long to prepare and you can experiment with no end of different fillings. This one right here, well, it tastes just great.

In a bowl mix the margarine and flour until it forms a smooth dough.

Divide the dough into four individual quiche trays or on an 8 inch round form baking tray.

In a pan fry the onions and garlic until tender.

Add the spring onion and leek and cook, stirring for about 4 minutes.

Then add the vegetable stock, pine nuts, tomatoes and black pepper and cook for a further 4 minutes.

Pour in the single cream and stir for 2 more minutes.

Divide the filling into the 4 individual quiche trays and bake them at 180°C for 30 minutes.

5 a Day Baked Rice

- 650g cooked rice
- 4 cloves of garlic smashed
- 1/2 large onion chopped
- 2 tbsp vegetable oil
- 250g closed cup chestnut mushrooms sliced
- 160g broccoli florets
- 2 handfuls of pitted green olives in brine, halved
- 1 tin of peas
- 15 cherry tomatoes halved
- 2 sticks of spring onion chopped
- 1 vegetable stock cube
- 45g pine nuts
- 2 handfuls of raisins
- black pepper to taste

Serves 6

PEAS

Peas have a high level of antioxidants and for that reason ensure a strong immune system and high energy levels. They also aid in the prevention of wrinkles, Alzheimer's, arthritis, bronchitis, osteoporosis and candida.

I call this "5 a Day Baked Rice" because the idea is to put as many vegetables in as possible, so in the end you have a healthy, rich and delicious meal which more than meets your RDA. You can't go wrong with this recipe; since I did it for the first time it's become something I cook every week as per my husband's request. I hope you enjoy it as much as we do!

Fry the garlic and the onion until tender.

Throw in the mushrooms and cook for 2 minutes.

Then add the broccoli and vegetable stock and cook for another 2 minutes.

Add the rest of the ingredients (apart from the rice), one at a time, stirring each one in for a bit before adding the next.

Cook until all the ingredients are tender.

Turn the heat off and add the rice, mixing it well.

Transfer the mixture to a baking tray and put it in the oven at 180°C for 25 minutes.

Mashed Surprise

- 700g potatoes
- 150ml vegan single cream
- 150g shimeji mushrooms
- 150g shiitake mushrooms
- 250g chestnut mushrooms
- 1/2 onion chopped
- 4 cloves of garlic crushed
- 1 vegetable stock cube
- 1 tbsp pine nuts
- 2 sticks of spring onion chopped
- black pepper
- 2 tbsp vegan margarine melted

Serves 4

SHIITAKE

Shiitake mushrooms reduce cholesterol, strengthen the immune system, help prevent cancer and thrombosis, are rich in iron, and also aid weight loss.

In Brazil this dish is called "escondidinho", and in England, Shepherd's Pie. Well, my version is neither, naturally, as it's vegan, but believe me it wins hands down. The good thing about this recipe is that you can take the filling in any direction you like - I love trying different ones but mushroom is without a doubt my favourite. See how you get on, and get creative!

Slice the potatoes and cook them in boiling salted water for about 15 minutes, or until a fork can easily be poked through them.

Drain the water, add the single cream and mash the potatoes until they are lump-free (unless you like a few lumps here and there of course).

In the meantime fry the garlic and onions until tender.

Add the rest of the ingredients apart from the margarine and cook for about 15 minutes, stirring occasionally.

Transfer the mushroom mixture to a baking dish and cover it completely with the mashed potato.

Brush the top of the mash with the melted margarine and bake it for 30 minutes at 200°C.

Tofu and Mushroom Stroganoff

- 2 cloves of garlic smashed
- 1/2 onion chopped
- 250g tofu cut into small cubes
- 250g chestnut mushrooms sliced
- 1 tsp paprika
- 1 tsp mustard
- 500ml vegan soya single cream
- 7 tbsp ketchup
- 2 tbsp vegetable oil
- black pepper to taste
- salt to taste

Serves 4

If you've always liked stroganoff this vegan version won't let you down, but rather open new doors. A hit at home every time, I guarantee it'll have you coming back for more.

Fry the garlic and the onion until tender.

Add the tofu and continue to fry, stirring for 7 minutes.

Throw in the mushrooms, paprika, mustard, salt and black pepper and stir for a further 9 minutes.

Pour in the cream and cook for just a few minutes more. Add the ketchup, mix it all together and serve.

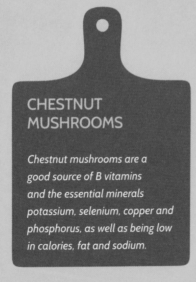

CHESTNUT MUSHROOMS

Chestnut mushrooms are a good source of B vitamins and the essential minerals potassium, selenium, copper and phosphorus, as well as being low in calories, fat and sodium.

Wild Mushroom Pie

Pastry
- 100g flour
- 50g wholemeal flour
- 100ml water
- 2 ½ tbsp vegetable oil
- 1 tsp salt

Filling
- 1 red onion cut into big chunks
- 2 cloves of garlic smashed
- 250g chestnut mushrooms sliced
- 100g wild mushrooms
- 3 sticks of spring onion chopped
- 200g tofu crumbled
- 1 vegetable stock cube
- 1 tbsp sesame oil

Serves 5

This tart is so yummy that it's a real blessing. The combination of ingredients gives you a delicious meal, full of healthy goodness, which goes just great with white rice and salad. I hope you find it as wholesome as we did!

Using your hands mix the pastry ingredients together into a soft-ball consistency.

Turn out onto a floured surface and knead for 5 minutes, until the dough is smooth and elastic. Cover it with cling film and let it rest for 30 minutes.

Open the dough out on a 7 or 8 inch round springform baking tray until at the top of the sides.

Fry the garlic and onion in a tablespoon of vegetable oil until tender.

Add the chestnut mushrooms, vegetable stock and spring onion and stir for about 5 minutes.

Throw in the wild mushrooms and the sesame oil and stir for a further 5 minutes.

Turn off the heat then add the tofu.

Pour the filling onto the baking tray and fold over the dough that's left into the middle.

Bake at 180°C for 30 minutes.

SESAME OIL

Sesame oil lowers the risk of high blood pressure and reduces plaque in artery walls, slows down the aging process, and improves immune system functioning by increasing levels of vitamin E, iron, and calcium.

Homemade Ravioli

Pasta
- 1 ⅔ cups pasta flour
- 2/3 cup of water
- 1 tbsp parsley and lime seasoning (optional)
- 3/4 tsp salt
- 1 tsp olive oil

Filling
- 1/2 onion thinly chopped
- 250g shimeji mushrooms
- 3 sticks of spring onion chopped
- 1 tbsp pine nuts
- 1 cup of vegetable stock
- black pepper

Serves 4

SPRING ONION

Spring onions are rich in nutrients including the vitamins A, B2, C, K, and thiamine. In addition to those, they are good sources of copper, phosphorous, magnesium, potassium, chromium, manganese and fibre. Spring onions are also a reliable source of flavonoids such as quercetin.

I was really proud of myself when I finished this recipe for the very first time. Opening the pasta is a real workout but it pays off in the end as this dish is heavenly, it has to be said. It's light and soft, but it also looks rather nice and fancy. It may seem a little complicated as there are so many steps, but it's not really, simply a bit time consuming. Just be sure to try this one when you have a bit of time to spend in the kitchen and believe you me, you will hear wows and yums galore when you're done.

PASTA

In a large bowl, combine the flour and salt, and then add the water.

Stir the mixture with a fork until it starts to form a ball. Then you can use your hands to combine the dough. If it's too dry, add more water; if it's too wet, add a little bit more flour.

Turn the ball of dough out onto a well-floured chopping board. You'll need to knead the dough for 10 minutes or so, or until it becomes smooth and pliable.

Let the dough rest, wrapped in cling film, for about 10 minutes.

FILLING

Fry the onion until tender.

Add the rest of the ingredients and stir for 10-15 minutes.

Let it cool down well before you start using it to fill the ravioli.

FILLING YOUR RAVIOLI

Divide the dough in three.

Using a rolling pin open the pasta right out until it's nice and thin.

Using an inverted small glass cut the pasta into little round circles.

Put 1 tablespoon of the filling in the middle of each ravioli, place a circle lid on top, and use a fork to close the edges nice and tight all around the outside.

COOKING YOUR RAVIOLI

Drop the raviolis (of which you should have around 15) in salted boiling water and cook until they rise to the surface.

Sprinkle olive oil, sea salt and vegan cheese on top, and serve.

Gnocchi

Gnocchi
- 1kg potatoes peeled and sliced
- 1 ½ cups flour plus extra for kneading and dusting
- salt

Tomato sauce
- 650g plum tomatoes halved
- 2 onions chopped
- 4 cloves of garlic
- 10g chives chopped
- 1 handful basil
- 1 vegetable stock cube
- black pepper
- 1 tbsp vegan margarine

Serves 5

BASIL

Basil may be a flavourful addition to our kitchen cuisine, but it's also rich in beta-carotene and other carotenoids, powerful antioxidants that protect cells from free radical damage and cholesterol. Basil is also an excellent source of magnesium, improving blood flow and promoting cardiovascular health and wellbeing.

Making your own gnocchi is far easier than you'd think. The secret is to cook them 4 or 5 at a time and sprinkle a little bit of water on the ones you've done while you cook the rest, to prevent them from sticking together.

GNOCCHI

Boil the potatoes for about 20 minutes until soft. Set aside until cool enough to handle, then mash well.

Add 1/2 cup of flour and work it all together using your hands.

Add the rest of the flour, a 1/2 cup at a time, and knead well to blend in all of the flour.

Transfer the dough onto a floured surface and knead for 2 minutes, adding a bit more flour if need be, but bear in mind the dough should be a bit sticky.

Divide the mixture into four and roll each one out into a 20mm diameter rope, then cut the strips at 15mm intervals.

Drop the gnocchi into boiling salted water and scoop them out when they rise to the top.

TOMATO SAUCE

Fry the garlic and onions over a low heat for 5 minutes.

Sprinkle in the chives and stir for about 5 minutes.

Add the tomatoes, black pepper, basil and vegetable stock and continue to cook with a low heat for a further 20 minutes.

When the pasta is ready, add the vegan margarine and mix it with the sauce.

Sunflower Seed Pesto Pasta

- 500g penne pasta
- 66g fresh basil
- 1/2 cup pine nuts
- 1 cup sunflower seeds
- 1/4 cup vegan cheese
- juice of 1 lime
- 3 cloves of garlic
- 1/2 cup olive oil
- salt
- black pepper

Serves 4

Pesto sauce is delicious, and this version is just like the "real" one. Nice and simple, this recipe is quite a treat!

Cook the pasta as per the package instructions.

When the pasta is almost done blend the rest of the ingredients thoroughly in a food processor.

Mix it all in well together and serve.

SUNFLOWER SEEDS

Sunflower seeds control cell damage, thus play a part in preventing cancer. This is because sunflower seeds are a good source of selenium, which is a proven enemy of cancer. They also contain bone-healthy minerals. Besides calcium, your bones need magnesium and copper to stay strong, and sunflower seeds have both of these minerals. As a bonus they also contain vitamin E, which helps ease arthritic pain.

"Ricotta" and Spinach Lasagne

- 9 lasagne sheets
- 250ml tomato sauce
- 400g tofu
- 1/4 cup almond milk
- 1 tbsp olive oil
- 3 cloves of garlic smashed
- 1/2 onion chopped
- juice of half a lemon
- 1 tbsp mustard
- 1 tbsp sugar
- 1/2 tbsp salt
- 120g baby spinach leaves
- 2 tbsp vegetable oil

Serves 6

SPINACH

Spinach is a good source of dietary fibre which aids digestion, prevents constipation, maintains low blood sugar and curbs overeating.

This lasagne is insanely delicious, and it's relatively quick and easy to prepare. There's no need to cook the lasagne sheets before you place it in the oven, and the tofu mixture tastes uncannily like ricotta, hence the name. Give it a try, you're gonna love it.

Fry the onions and 2 cloves of garlic in the vegetable oil until tender.

Add the tomato sauce, sugar, mustard and a small amount of water and bring it to the boil.

In a food processor beat the tofu, almond milk, olive oil, 1 clove of garlic, lemon juice and salt for a few seconds, just enough to incorporate all the ingredients together.

Add the spinach leaves to the tofu "ricotta" mixture.

Spoon a bit of the tomato sauce into the bottom of the baking dish and place the pasta sheets on top, then spread half of the ricotta/spinach mixture out evenly using a spatula, and pour on more of the tomato sauce.

Repeat the process until the final layer of pasta and tomato sauce.

Bake in a preheated oven at 180°C for 45 minutes.

Aubergine a La Parmigiana

Aubergine
- 2 aubergines sliced
- 1 jar of tomato sauce
- 3 sticks of spring onion chopped
- 3 cloves of garlic
- 1/2 onion chopped
- 1 tbsp mustard
- 2 tbsp sugar
- salt
- black pepper

Cream cheese
- 250g tofu
- 1/2 cup olive oil
- 2 tsp salt
- juice of 1 lime
- 1 tbsp cornflour
- 1 tbsp water
- black pepper

Serves 4

AUBERGINE

Aubergines are very low in calories and fats but rich in soluble fibre content. This vegetable is also a good source of minerals like manganese, copper, iron and potassium.

I simply adore aubergines, and in this regard a la parmigiana is my favourite. This is what comfort food should taste like; serve it with rice and salad, and you have something special!

AUBERGINE

Boil the aubergines in salted water for about 15 minutes, until they start to go translucent, which means they've lost most of their water.

In a separate pan fry the garlic and onions until tender.

Add the tomato sauce, spring onion, mustard, sugar and black pepper. (I normally add sugar with tinned tomato sauce as it tends to be too acidic for my taste).

CREAM CHEESE

Blend the tofu and the olive oil.

Transfer the mixture to a pan and add the rest of the ingredients.

Stir steadily over a low flame until it's almost at boiling point, but don't let it boil.

COOKING

Place the aubergines in a baking tray and spread the cream cheese over them evenly.

Pour on the tomato sauce and bake it for 30 minutes in a preheated oven at 180°C

Chocolate and Blueberry Cake

Cake (ingredients per layer)
- 115g raw cane sugar
- 4 tsp unsweetened cocoa powder
- 1/2 tsp salt
- 170g flour
- 1 tsp baking soda
- 90ml vegetable oil
- 1 tsp vanilla extract
- 2 tsp white cider vinegar
- 200ml cold water

Ganache
- 150g dark chocolate
- 250ml vegan single cream, warmed
- 2 tsp port wine

Topping
- 200g blueberries

Serves 10

BLUEBERRIES

Blueberries, being very rich in antioxidants like anthocyanin, vitamins A, B complex, C and E, copper, selenium, zinc and iron, boost up your immune system and help prevent infections. Once your immunity is strong, you won't catch colds or fevers and all such nasty viral and bacterially-communicable diseases.

This is one of those cakes that tastes as good as it looks, if not a whole lot better; it's opulent, rich and absolutely divine. There's no rational way round it - you simply have to try it.

CAKE

Mix the sugar, cocoa, salt, flour and baking soda in a big bowl.

Add the oil, vanilla essence and vinegar and pour the cold water over the mixture.

Combine well with a fork, but do not beat it.

Pour the mixture into a greased springform baking tray and bake it at 180°C for 20-30 minutes.

Once done, wait for the cake to cool completely before removing it from the baking tray, and then repeat the recipe one more time (or do both layers at the same time if you can).

GANACHE

Melt the chocolate in a microwave or a bain-marie.

Pour in the warm vegan single cream and stir.

Add the port and then place it in the fridge for 30 minutes to set.

PUTTING THE CAKE TOGETHER

Spread half of the ganache on top of the first cake layer (i.e. the base) and put it in the fridge for 20 minutes.

Put the second layer on top of the first, and spread the rest of the ganache on top of this.

Blanket the surface of the cake with blueberries, and carefully dust it with icing sugar.

Place it in the fridge for 30 minutes before serving.

Chocolate Cheesecake

Base
- 13 vegan digestive biscuits crushed
- 1/2 cup vegan margarine melted

Filling
- 420g firm tofu
- 250g dark chocolate melted
- 6 tbsp unsweetened cocoa powder mixed with 100ml water (blend it together well to make a paste)
- 4 tbsp agave syrup
- 1 tbsp sugar
- 70g shredded almonds for topping

Serves 10

ALMONDS

Almonds reduce the risk of heart attack, lower 'bad' cholesterol, protect artery walls from damage, help build strong bones and teeth, provide healthy fats and aid weight loss, lower the rise in blood sugar and insulin after meals, help support good brain functioning, nourish the nervous system and alkalise the body.

This "cheesecake" is so delicious that you won't quite believe it's vegan. A sophisticated dessert that melts in your mouth, it's rich, chocolatey and rather heavenly. Indulge yourself!

BASE

Grease an 8 inch round springform baking tray.

Crumble the biscuits in a food processor.

Mix it thoroughly with the melted margarine and spread the biscuit base mixture evenly across the baking tin, pressing it down firmly with your fingers.

FILLING

Put the tofu in the food processor and blend it until smooth.

Add the rest of the ingredients one at a time and beat it until all the ingredients are nicely blended in.

Using a spatula pour the filling onto the base and sprinkle the chopped almonds on top of the cheesecake.

Cover with tin foil and place in the fridge overnight, or alternatively in the freezer for about 3 hours, before serving.

Chocolate Brownie

- 2 cups unbleached all-purpose flour
- 2 cups light brown sugar
- 3/4 cup unsweetened cocoa powder
- 1 tsp baking powder
- 1 tsp salt
- 1 cup water
- 1 cup vegetable oil
- 1 tsp vanilla extract

Serves 12

VANILLA EXTRACT

Vanilla extract helps with nausea, weight loss, reduces anxiety and stress, helps with healing of wounds and regulates menstruation.

Whenever people say that vegan food is bland I think of this brownie, and smile to myself. This cake is smooth and crunchy at the same time - utter bliss.

In a large bowl, mix together the flour, sugar, cocoa powder, baking powder and salt.

Pour in the water, vegetable oil and vanilla, and mix until blended well.

Spread the mixture evenly in a 9×13 inch baking pan.

Bake for 25-30 minutes in a preheated oven at 170°C or until the top is no longer shiny.

Let cool for at least 10 minutes (i.e. resist the temptation to eat it straight away), before cutting into squares ready to serve.

Prestigio (Bounty) Cake

Cake (ingredients per layer)
- 115g raw cane sugar
- 4 tsp unsweetened cocoa powder
- 1/2 tsp salt
- 170g flour
- 1 tsp baking soda
- 90ml vegetable oil
- 1 tsp vanilla essence
- 2 tsp cider vinegar
- 200ml cold water

Filling
- 1/2 can of coconut milk
- 1 cup desiccated coconut
- 1 tbsp cornflour
- 5 tbsp sugar

Icing
- 55g vegan margarine
- 30g unsweetened cocoa powder
- 4 tbsp almond milk
- 140g sugar
- 1 tsp vanilla extract

Serves 10

Prestigio is a small Brazilian chocolate bar which, very much like its UK equivalent of the bar Bounty, has a coconut filling encased with a layer of chocolate. I made this cake for the first time for my husband's birthday and as expected it was a hit, purely out of luck mind you as I had invented the filling on the same day! This cake is rich and delicious - a real treat!

CAKE

Mix the sugar, cocoa, salt, flour and baking soda in a large bowl.

Add the oil, vanilla essence and vinegar and pour the cold water over the mixture.

Combine well with a fork, but do not beat.

Pour into a greased round springform baking tray and bake at 180°C for 20-30 minutes.

Once baked, wait for the cake to cool down before removing from the baking tray and then repeat the recipe to make the other half of the cake (or do both at the same time if possible).

FILLING

Mix 3 tablespoons of the coconut milk with the cornflour.

Combine the rest of the ingredients in a saucepan and bring them to the boil over a low heat, slowly, stirring constantly.

Let it cool down a bit before you apply it to the top of the first cake.

ICING

Combine all the ingredients (apart from the vanilla extract) in a saucepan and gradually bring to the boil, again, stirring constantly.

Remove from the heat, add the vanilla extract and stir to cool down a bit.

Spread the icing on top of the cake and you're done.

Apricot Chocolate Tart

- 200g flour
- 110g vegan margarine
- 1 tbsp sugar
- 250g dried apricots
- 400ml coconut milk
- 10 tbsp light brown sugar
- 2 tbsp cornflour
- 1 cup sweetened coconut flakes
- 100g dark chocolate
- 250ml vegan single cream

Serves 8

APRICOT

The variety of nutrients found in apricots is very beneficial for good eyesight and also helps to prevent heart disease and other ailments. Apricots are also rich in powerful antioxidants such as lycopene, helping to promote wellness and strengthen the immune system. The healthy fruit is also a good source of fibre, which is of course beneficial for healthy digestion.

Chocolate goes really well with apricot - throw coconut into the mix too and you're verging on perfection. Sophisticated and rich, you're sure to impress your friends with this tart.

Bring the flour, vegan margarine and sugar together into a dough.

Open the dough on an 18cm round springform baking pan and place it in the oven for 30 minutes at 180°C.

In a saucepan cook the apricot for 15 minutes using just enough water to cover it.

Once the apricots soften, drain the water saving 4 tablespoons worth, and beat the fruit in a multiprocessor until it becomes a paste.

Mix the 4 tablespoons of the apricot water with the cornflour.

In a saucepan mix the coconut milk, light brown sugar and coconut flakes. Add the cornflour mixture and stir for 15 minutes.

Let it cool down and then beat together with the apricot paste for a good 2 minutes.

Melt the chocolate in a microwave (or in a bain-marie) and mix it with the single cream.

Take the tart shell from the pan, pour on the apricot mixture and place it in the fridge for 15 minutes.

Carefully pour the chocolate ganache on top of the tart and leave it in the fridge overnight.

Brazilian "Honey" Cake

- 250g light brown sugar
- 1 cup water
- 2 ¼ cups flour
- 1/2 cup golden syrup
- 1/2 tsp nutmeg
- 1/2 tsp cinnamon
- 1 tbsp cocoa powder
- 1/2 tbsp baking soda
- 1/2 cup almond milk
- 100g vegan "milk" chocolate
- 100g dark chocolate

Serves 15

NUTMEG

Nutmeg can effectively stimulate your brain. As a result, it can help eliminate fatigue and stress. If you are suffering from anxiety or depression, nutmeg may also be a good remedy. It can also improve your concentration, so you can be more efficient and focused at work or at school.

This is a traditional cake in Brazil – as the name suggests, it's normally made with honey, but I use golden syrup instead and even my friends find it better than the "real" one. Sweet, chocolatey and ridiculously moreish, it's an absolute delight.

Mix all the dried ingredients, add the syrup and set to one side.

In a saucepan add the sugar to the water and stir continuously for 18 minutes over a medium heat or until it begins to thicken a bit – whichever happens first – but be very careful not to leave it over the heat for too long otherwise it will crystallise.

Turn off the heat without stopping stirring and pour the caramel mixture in with the rest of the ingredients.

Add the almond milk and mix well.

Pour the mixture into a greased and floured baking tray and place it in a preheated oven at 180°C for 30 minutes.

Once baked, remove from the oven and let it cool completely. Remove from the baking tray and cut the cake into small squares.

Melt the chocolate and dip the top of the squares in it, then allow the chocolate to harden, and serve.

Passion Fruit Cheesecake

Crust
- 1 cup walnuts
- 1/2 cup almonds flakes
- 3 tbsp vegan margarine melted

Filling
- 3 cups of cashews soaked overnight
- 1/2 cup lemon juice
- 3 cups golden syrup
- 2 tsp vanilla extract
- 3 cups coconut oil
- 3 tbsp cornflour
- 3 tbsp light brown sugar

Topping
- 1 cup passion fruit
- 4 tbsp light brown sugar
- 4 tbsp water
- 1 tbsp cornflour

Serves 8

PASSION FRUIT

Passion fruit contains iron, magnesium and calcium, and has a soporific effect on the human nervous system that creates a sense of calm and helps you to relax.

This is one of my all-time favourite desserts. It's suave, light and delicate, yet full of healthy ingredients. So if you like nuts, and passion, and fruit, then this one's for you!

CRUST

In a food processor mix the ingredients of the crust and spread it, pressing down with your fingers, in a greased 8 inch round springform baking tray. If you wish to take the cheesecake out of the baking tray after, then place a layer of greased baking paper underneath the crust.

FILLING

Drain the cashews and blend them in a food processor for about 2 minutes.

If your coconut oil is not liquid, melt it in a microwave for 1 minute.

Then, one at a time, add the rest of the filling ingredients to the food processor, apart from the cornflour and coconut oil, and beat for about 10 minutes.

Only stop when all of the ingredients are mixed together well to form a thick cream.

Melt the coconut oil and add the cornflour to it, making sure it dissolves.

Add the mixture to the blend in the food processor and beat for another 2 minutes.

Pour the mixture on top of the crust and spread it as evenly as you can, then place it in the freezer for 1 hour.

TOPPING

Put the passion fruit and sugar in a saucepan over a low heat.

Mix the cornflour with the water and add it to the pan.

Stir until it thickens, let it cool for a moment, and then pour on top of the cheesecake.

Leave the cake in the freezer for about 6 hours, and take it out 1-2 hours before you wish to serve it.

Apple Strudel

- 1 Royal Gala apple thinly sliced
- 1 tbsp cinnamon
- 2 tbsp light brown sugar
- 4 tbsp raisins
- 3/4 tbsp all purpose flour
- juice of half a lime
- 1/2 sheet of vegan puff pastry
- 1/2 tsp vegan margarine melted

Serves 6

APPLE

An apple a day not only keeps doctors away, but they help give whiter, healthier teeth, a healthier heart, avoid Alzheimer's, protect against Parkinson's, decrease the risk of diabetes and reduce cholesterol. They also prevent gallstones, beat diarrhoea and constipation, neutralise irritable bowel syndrome, detoxify your liver, boost your immune system and prevent cataracts!

I'd always thought strudel to be the most difficult dessert to make, but if you use readymade pastry it's a whole lot easier - I know it's cheating, but what can I say! Delicate, heavenly, sweet... I can't emphasise enough how good this recipe is.

Defrost the pastry overnight in the fridge.

In a bowl mix the apple, the lime juice and the raisins.

In another bowl combine the cinnamon, sugar and flour.

Mix the fruit in with the dried ingredients.

Place the mixture in a line down the middle of the pastry on a baking tray.

Fold the dough over and tuck in the ends.

Brush the strudel with the melted margarine and give it a generous dusting of sugar.

Bake it at 150°C for 40 minutes.

Banana Cake

- 2 cups plain flour
- 1 ½ cups light brown sugar
- 1 tbsp baking powder
- 1/2 cup vegetable oil
- 1 tbsp vegan single cream
- 3/4 cup almond milk
- 4 bananas thinly sliced
- 1 tbsp cinnamon

Serves 10

BANANA

Bananas help combat
depression due to high levels of
tryptophan, which is converted
into serotonin, the happy-mood
brain neurotransmitter.

Picture a warm Spring day, you relaxing watching an old chick flick movie on TV or reading your favourite novel, and next to you is a tray with a cuppa and a slice of the best cake ever. In my opinion, this is that very cake. Banana is one of those fruits that is delicious any which way you have it - mashed, baked, with cinnamon or ice-cream - and this recipe says it all really.

In a large bowl mix the flour, sugar and baking powder.

Add the oil, vegan single cream, almond milk and cinnamon and mix thoroughly.

Add the bananas and mix well.

Bake in a greased and floured tube pan for 45 minutes in a preheated oven at 180°C, then pick out your favourite film or novel, pop the kettle on and relax.

Strawberry Pie

Crust
- 1 ¼ cups all-purpose flour
- 8 tbsp vegan margarine
- 2 tbsp light brown sugar
- ice cold water

Strawberry filling
- 400g strawberries sliced
- 1/4 cup light brown sugar
- 1/2 tsp cinnamon
- 1 ½ tbsp cornstarch
- 1 tsp vanilla

Serves 6

STRAWBERRY

One cup of strawberries contains only 43 calories. The fruit is rich in the B-complex group of vitamins, has fibre that helps lower blood pressure, and curbs overeating. They contain very good amounts of vitamin B-6, niacin, riboflavin, pantothenic acid and folic acid. Strawberries also have potassium, vitamin K and magnesium, which are important for healthy bones.

This recipe is not exactly difficult, it's just time-consuming, but is totally worth it. Words can barely do justice how lovely and tasty the pie is; its crust is crumbly, the filling rich and moist, and all this with just the right amount of sweetness.

CRUST

Place all the ingredients except the water in a bowl and, using a fork, mix them well.

Then slowly, one tablespoon at a time, drizzle the cold water on and mix it all quickly with the fork until the dough starts to come together and fall away from the sides of the bowl.

Divide the dough in two, one part slightly bigger than the other, and wrap them in cling film, shaping into discs as you go.

Place both dough discs in the fridge for 1 hour.

STRAWBERRY FILLING

Mix in all the ingredients and stir gently.

Set aside for 15 minutes.

PUTTING THE PIE TOGETHER

Take the bigger disc from the fridge and roll it out to about 12 inches, using as much flour as you need to keep it from sticking to the work surface, and keep moving the dough as you roll it to ensure it does not stick.

Open the dough out on a greased 8 inch round springform pie pan.

Pour the filling into the crust and place the pan in the fridge while you prepare the top crust using the second disc of dough.

Open the second disc and use a small cookie cutter (of any shape you wish) to cut out little pieces of the dough.

Arrange the shapes on top of the strawberries in a decorative pattern.

Sprinkle 1 tablespoon of light brown sugar on the crust. This gives some additional sweetness and helps the crust to brown.

Bake it at 180ºC for 1 hour.

When it's done let the pan cool thoroughly before cutting the pie up and serving.

Éclair

Whipped cream
- 1 cup cashew nuts
- 3 tbsp golden syrup
- 1/4 cup vegan margarine
- 6 tbsp water
- 1 tsp vanilla extract

Chocolate topping
- 100g dark chocolate
- 150ml vegan single cream

Éclair
- 1 sheet of puff pastry

Serves 6

Éclairs are light and divine and this vegan version is no exception to the rule. I tend to use puff pastry as I like it to be a little bit crispy. The cashew whipped cream is to die for, and is something you can use in all sorts of other recipes.

Take a small upside down glass and cut circles out of the pastry. Group the remaining pastry, roll it and repeat this step, so as not to waste any.

Using the back of a teaspoon or a wooden spoon lightly press the centre of the circles and bake them at 170°C for 25 minutes.

In the meantime mix all the ingredients of the whipped cream in a food processor and then beat for a minimum of 5 minutes or until the mixture turns smooth, creamy, and slightly fluffy.

Melt the chocolate in the microwave and mix with the single cream.

When the pastry is swollen and golden brown, remove it from the oven and, using a sharp knife, cut along the middle to open it.

You will see that there's a line on the side and that only by pressing in a knife will you be able to open it easily.

Put 2 tablespoons of the whipped cream on the base of the shells, dunk the top in the chocolate cream and close them, pressing down lightly.

Put the éclairs in the fridge to chill for at least 1 hour before serving.

CASHEW NUTS

Cashews are particularly rich in magnesium. It's a well-known fact that calcium is necessary for strong bones, but so too is magnesium, as most of the magnesium in the human body is in our bones. Some of it helps lend bones their physical structure, and the remainder is located on the surface of the bone where it is stored for the body to use as it needs. Copper found in cashews is vital for the function of enzymes involved in combining collagen and elastin, providing substance and flexibility in bones and joints.

Apple Crumble

- *3 apples thinly sliced*
- *1 tbsp sugar*
- *4 tbsp water*
- *105g vegan margarine*
- *170g flour*
- *55g light brown sugar*
- *55g sugar*
- *1 tbsp cinnamon*
- *4 tbsp sliced almonds*
- *4 tbsp oats*

Serves 6

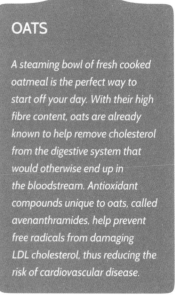

OATS

A steaming bowl of fresh cooked oatmeal is the perfect way to start off your day. With their high fibre content, oats are already known to help remove cholesterol from the digestive system that would otherwise end up in the bloodstream. Antioxidant compounds unique to oats, called avenanthramides, help prevent free radicals from damaging LDL cholesterol, thus reducing the risk of cardiovascular disease.

Apple crumble is not only warm and yummy but it's extremely easy and quick to prepare too. The oats and almond slices in this one make all the difference - you'll really love this recipe!

Mix the apples with the water and sugar and pour the mixture into an ovenproof dish.

In big bowl combine all the topping ingredients together, then pile the crumble on top of the apple and sugar mixture.

Bake at 150°C for 45 minutes.

Flan with Walnut Crumbs

- 1 tsp powdered agar
- 1 cup + 1 tbsp almond milk
- 1 cup vegan single cream
- 1/4 cup light brown sugar
- 1 tsp vanilla extract
- 2 tbsp water
- 200g white sugar
- 200g walnuts

Serves 5

WALNUTS

Regular consumption of walnuts would protect against cardiovascular disease in the long run. They are rich in monounsaturated fatty acids like oleic acid and are an excellent source of all important omega-3 essential fatty acids. In addition, they are an excellent source of vitamin E, manganese, copper, potassium, calcium, iron, magnesium, zinc, and selenium.

This flan is wonderfully fresh and light. It takes next to no time to prepare and is just lush. The crumbs made of praline walnuts are spot on, and the combination of the two is just awesome.

WALNUT PRALINE

In a saucepan add the water and white sugar and cook it until it turns golden brown. When doing this don't use a spoon to mix the water and sugar - use a frying pan with a handle and gently swill the mixture in the pan.

Add the walnuts to the caramel then mix with a wooden spoon.

Transfer the mixture to a greased sheet of baking paper, cover with another sheet and roll it with a rolling pin.

Let it cool completely, then transfer to a food processor and break it up into crumbs.

You'll get a lot more than you need for this recipe but don't worry, it goes wonderfully with fruit or ice cream.

FLAN

Place the agar in a small saucepan, mix it with 1 tablespoon of almond milk, and stir continuously until dissolved.

Add the remaining almond milk, single cream and sugar. Bring to the boil over a medium to high heat, stirring constantly to help dissolve the sugar.

Boil for about 30 seconds - if the mixture threatens to bubble over, briefly remove it from the heat until the foam subsides.

After 30 seconds, remove from the heat, let cool for about 3 minutes and divide evenly into 4 ramekins or cocktail glasses.

Cover with some cling film and refrigerate for at least 30 minutes.

Sprinkle the crumbs on top of the flan, and serve.

Chocolate Truffles

- 1/2 cup almond milk
- 1 tbsp margarine
- 2 tbsp sugar
- 2 tbsp unsweetened cocoa powder
- 400g dark chocolate

Serves 8

DARK CHOCOLATE

Dark chocolate is good for your heart and brain. It helps control blood sugar, is full of antioxidants and has high concentrations of potassium, copper, iron and magnesium.

These truffles are divine, and they go perfectly with grapes and strawberries. They're chocolatey (naturally), melt in your mouth, and will impress even your biggest meat-eating friends. Give them a try, I can guarantee you won't regret it!

Mix all the ingredients together in a small pan.

Stir constantly over a low heat until the chocolate melts and it becomes a smooth cream.

While stirring, if you think that it's getting too hot just take the pan off the heat and keep stirring.

Leave the mixture in the fridge for about 2 hours to allow it to firm up.

Using your hands make small balls and roll them on unsweetened cocoa powder.

Homemade Mint Chocolates

- 8 tbsp virgin coconut oil
- 10 tbsp icing sugar
- 6 tbsp unsweetened cocoa powder
- 4 tsp peppermint extract
- 2 tbsp chopped hazelnuts

MINT

Mint's health benefits include soothing the digestive tract, reducing irritated bowel syndrome (by drinking it as herbal tea), cleansing the stomach and also clearing up skin disorders such as acne. It also helps in eliminating toxins from the body, to whiten teeth and to combat bad breath.

How can I describe these treats – rich, smooth, chocolatey, exquisite, absolutely yummy and even so, none of those come even close to spelling out how good they really are. It's one of those things that we can't make often unfortunately as they're very fattening, but believe me it's worth every bite, leaving a sweet-bitter taste in your mouth which is wonderful. The good thing, however, is that you know exactly what you're eating.

I like to sprinkle my chocolates with hazelnuts, but you can embellish them with anything you like: coconut, almonds, sunflower seeds, the sky's the limit...

Melt the coconut oil in a bain-marie or in a microwave. If you do the latter it will probably only take 1 minute to melt, but rather than doing it for 1 minute it's best to put it in twice for 30 seconds each time.

Stir in the sugar and cocoa until it's smooth.

Add the peppermint extract and stir a bit more.

Lay a sheet of baking paper in two bread tins and pour half of the liquid chocolate into each tin.

Sprinkle the chopped hazelnuts on top of the chocolate and place it in the fridge for 30 minutes.

Remove the chocolate bars from the tin and you're done, but if it doesn't all go straight away be sure to keep it sealed and in the fridge to prevent it from melting.

Strawberry Mille-feuille

- 1 sheet vegan puff pastry
- 400g strawberries sliced
- 4 tbsp light brown sugar
- icing sugar for dusting

Whipped cream
- 2 cups cashew nuts
- 6 tbsp golden syrup
- 1/4 cup vegan margarine
- 6 tbsp water
- 1 tsp vanilla extract

Serves 6

The word that comes to my mind when I think about these treats is perfection! They're light, sweet - but not too sweet - the whipped cream and strawberry mixture is divine and the whole dessert is sheer heaven really. You simple have to try it, and believe me, you'll thank me later!

Open the dough and cut it into small rectangles. I simply used a small plastic food container upside down, and it worked a treat.

Arrange the squares on a baking tray in between two sheets of baking paper, and place a heavy baking tray on top to prevent them from puffing up.

Bake for 25 minutes at 180°C.

In the meantime mix all the ingredients of the whipped cream in a food processor and beat it for a minimum of 5 minutes or until the mixture becomes smooth, creamy, and slightly fluffy.

Mix the sugar in with the strawberries and set to one side.

When the pastry is baked and golden brown, take a knife and divide each rectangle in two by cutting in horizontally from the side through the middle of the pastry - you'll need three of these thin pastry slices to make one mille-feuile.

Spread 2 tablespoons of the whipped cream on the base shell, then place 2 tablespoons of the strawberry mixture on the cream.

Repeat the process with the cream and strawberries on the middle shell of pastry, put this on the first one, and then seal it with the third one placed on top of the other two, pressing it down gently.

Dust with a little icing sugar and serve them straight away.

Double Chocolate Muffin

Muffin
- *2 cups flour*
- *3/4 cup unsweetened cocoa powder*
- *1 tbsp baking powder*
- *1 cup light brown sugar*
- *1/2 tsp salt*
- *1 ¾ cups almond milk*
- *1/2 cup vegetable oil*
- *1 tsp vanilla extract*
- *1 cup vegan chocolate chips*
- *1 tbsp water*

Walnut Praline (optional)
- *200g walnuts*
- *100g white sugar*
- *100ml water*

Serves 12

This recipe is about as chocolatey and rich as it gets. Soft and light, it's one of those treats you simply can't get enough of.

MUFFIN

In a large bowl stir together the flour, cocoa powder, baking powder, salt and light brown sugar.

Add the almond milk, oil, vanilla extract and the chocolate chips.

Spoon the mixture evenly onto a greased muffin tin and bake it for 16 minutes at 200°C, or until a fork comes out clean when inserted.

WALNUT PRALINE

See page 81

Coconut Dreams

- 1 cup desiccated coconut
- 1/8 cup light brown sugar
- 1/8 cup golden syrup
- 1 tsp vanilla extract
- 100g dark chocolate
- 2 tbsp vegan single cream warmed

COCONUT

Coconut is highly nutritious and rich in fibre, vitamins, and minerals. It is classified as a "functional food" because it provides many health benefits beyond its nutritional content, boosting energy and endurance, and enhancing physical and athletic performance. Coconut also improves digestion and absorption of other nutrients including vitamins, minerals, and amino acids.

This is what a real treat tastes like, and that's something we all need from time to time, right? Well, if you manage to resist and keep your hands away from a few of these babies why not wrap them up and give them to someone special...

In a small bowl mix the coconut, sugar, golden syrup and vanilla extract.

Place the mixture in the fridge and let it stand for at least one hour.

Take it out and make little balls using a tablespoon, then put them back in the fridge for another hour.

Melt the chocolate in a microwave (or a bain-marie) and add the single cream.

Dunk the coconut balls into the chocolate and transfer them to a sheet of baking paper.

Leave in the fridge overnight to set.

Shortbread

- 230g vegan margarine
- 125g light brown sugar
- 1 tsp vanilla extract
- 300g plain flour

I've always liked shortbread, so I thought I'd have a crack at veganising it. Truth be told I wasn't expecting it to be *this* good, as I always thought shortbread was all about the butter, but it turns out - and I'm sure you've noticed a pattern emerging here - that I ended up liking this one more than the old recipe. A tasty classic nibble to go with a cuppa - you won't be disappointed.

Cream the margarine and the sugar until light and fluffy.

Add vanilla extract and 250g of flour, a little at a time, and incorporate until the dough is smooth. Wrap the dough in cling film and place it in the fridge to chill for 30 minutes.

Using the rest of the flour, knead the dough on a flat surface and then roll out to a thickness of just under 1cm.

Cut the biscuits with a cookie cutter and place them on a baking tray covered with a sheet of baking paper.

Preheat the oven to 170°C and bake the biscuits for 20 minutes or until they are golden brown.

Mint Chocolate Biscuits

- 1 ¼ cups all-purpose flour
- 1 cup light brown sugar
- 1/2 cup cocoa powder
- 1/4 tsp salt
- 1/4 tsp baking soda
- 3/4 cup vegan margarine
- 3 tbsp almond milk
- 1 tsp vanilla extract
- 3 tsp peppermint extract
- 100g dark chocolate
- 100g vegan milk chocolate

This is one of the best biscuit recipes I've ever baked. It's rich, chocolatey and super tasty. The flavour of the mint isn't too overbearing, but it's strong enough for you to know it's there. Ideal for one of those days when all you want is to put your feet up with a good book and something to treat yourself with.

In a large bowl combine the dry ingredients.

Add the remaining ingredients and knead it until it comes together and all the flour is incorporated. Add a bit more flour if needs be.

Wrap the dough in cling film and chill for 1 hour.

Preheat the oven to 180°C.

Roll a heaped teaspoon of cookie dough into a ball and place onto pre-prepared baking sheets.

Flatten the balls of dough evenly with your fingertips so that they're about a 1/4 inch thick, and bake for 12-14 minutes.

Remove from the oven, and when the biscuits have cooled down completely, melt the chocolate in a bain-marie and dunk half of each biscuit into the chocolate and place them on greaseproof paper.

Allow the chocolate to set and serve.

Banana "Honey" Biscuits

- 150g vegan margarine
- 100g light brown sugar
- 40g mashed banana
- 1 tsp vanilla extract
- 3 tbsp golden syrup
- 300g plain flour
- 1/2 tsp baking powder
- 1 tsp cinnamon

You won't believe how easy to prepare and good these biscuits are. Absolutely delicious with tea or coffee, it's the perfect accompaniment for an afternoon cuppa with friends!

Cooking times may vary according to the size of your cutter, so do be sure to check on them halfway through, just in case.

Beat together the sugar and the vegan margarine until pale and creamy.

Add the banana, vanilla extract and golden syrup.

Mix well then sift in the flour, baking powder and cinnamon.

Use your hands to bring it together into a dough, then allow to chill in the fridge for 1 hour.

Roll out the dough onto a lightly floured surface, to a thickness of about 3-4mm.

Cut out the biscuits using your favourite cutter, then carefully transfer them to a baking paper-lined tray and put them in the oven for about 10 minutes at 160°C.

Strawberry Delight Cookies

- *1 cup flour*
- *3 tbsp light brown sugar*
- *1 tsp salt*
- *70g vegan margarine*
- *1 tbsp water*
- *1 tsp vanilla extract*
- *80g strawberries cut into small cubes*
- *2 tbsp icing sugar to sprinkle*

These biscuits are a little slice of heaven, simply perfect. The light brown sugar enhances the flavour of the strawberries and the cookie has just the right amount of sweetness. You have to try making them, and that's all I have to say.

Combine the flour, salt and 2 tablespoons of sugar in a food processor.

Add the margarine and pulse until crumbs begin to form.

Pour in the water and vanilla and pulse a bit more to bring the dough together. Cover with cling film and let it stand for 15 minutes.

Mix the strawberries with the rest of the sugar and set aside.

On a floured surface open the dough using a rolling pin and cut into small squares. I simply use a small upside down plastic food container.

Lay a teaspoon of the strawberry mixture in the middle of each square, fold two opposite corners of the pastry together into the middle and press down gently with your fingers.

Bake in a preheated oven at 180°C for 15 minutes.

Sprinkle the icing sugar on top of the cookies while still hot.

"Cheese" Crackers

- 300g flour
- 200g vegan margarine
- 1 tbsp ground flaxseed
- 3 tbsp water
- 1 tsp salt
- 100g vegan Cheddar cheese
- 50g vegan Gouda cheese
- 1/2 tsp nutmeg

This recipe was inspired by a non-vegan one my sister-in-law has been doing for years, which I decided to veganise. The crackers are light, tasty and perfect as a snack or for a party. The only problem is how to hold back from eating them!

In a small pot mix the flaxseed and the water well and let it rest for 15 minutes or until it becomes gooey.

Mix all the ingredients together in a big bowl - you'll need to use your hands at some point during the preparation.

Leave the mixture to stand in the fridge for 30-40 minutes.

Using a dough roller open the dough out and cut it using a small round cookie cutter.

Bake the crackers at 180°C for 15 minutes or until golden brown.

Coconut "Sequilho" Biscuits

- 150g grated coconut
- 3 ½ cups cornflour
- 3 tbsp flaxseed
- 9 tbsp water
- 1 cup vegan margarine
- 1 ¾ cups light brown sugar

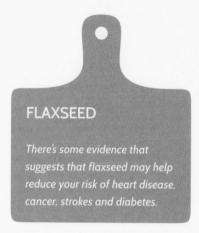

FLAXSEED

There's some evidence that suggests that flaxseed may help reduce your risk of heart disease, cancer, strokes and diabetes.

Sequilho is a typical Brazilian biscuit. It's light, sweet and wholly addictive - a perfect combination with tea or coffee.

Mix the flaxseed and the water and let it rest for 15 minutes or until it turns gooey.

Blend the flaxseed mixture together with the rest of the ingredients and knead until the dough forms a ball. If it gets too sticky add a little bit more cornflour.

On a floured surface shape small portions of the dough into long "snakes", and then cut them into 1.5cm strips.

Bake them in a preheated oven at 180°C for 15 minutes, and enjoy!

Index by Health Tips

Almonds	66	Lemon	43	Sesame Seeds	8
Apple	74	Lentils	45	Shimeji Mushrooms	25
Apricot	70	Macadamia nuts	10	Shiitake Mushrooms	53
Aubergine	62	Melon	20	Spinach	61
Avocado	22	Mint	83	Spring Onion	57
Balsamic Vinegar	47	Nutmeg	71	Strawberry	76
Banana	75	Oats	79	Sunflower Seeds	59
Basil	58	Olives	13	Tapioca	14
Black Eyed Beans	18	Onion	26	Tofu	46
Blueberries	65	Paprika	28	Tomato	30
Broccoli	39	Parsley	48	Vanilla Extract	67
Brown Rice	35	Passion Fruit	73	Walnuts	81
Carrot	27	Peas	51		
Cashew nuts	78	Pineapple	42		
Chestnut Mushrooms	54	Portobello Mushrooms	36		
Chives	31	Potato	38		
Coconut	87	Quinoa	23		
Courgette	33	Raisins	19		
Dark Chocolate	82	Red Lentils	34		
Flaxseed	95	Red Onion	41		
Green Beans	17	Rosemary	9		
Leek	50	Sesame Oil	55		